To Eva, Christian, and Bjorn:
my heart, my soul, my inspiration.

WALTER IOOSS

A LIFETIME SHOOTING SPORTS & BEAUTY

Photographs by Walter Iooss
Foreword: Russell Drumm
Book Design: B. Martin Pedersen, Massimo Acanfora

Published by Graphis Inc.

"I've always felt the moment. People call me lucky, and luck is a wonderful attribute. But it's more — it's a sense somehow. It's inexplicable, it happens. It's a feeling and you just move into that direction. Someone once said that wherever I am is the perfect picture. I didn't like the way it sounded, but I believe that. It's not that I'm positive of it deep down inside, it's that I have to believe it. When you make that decision — 'this is the place to go' — you've got to live with it. There's no alternative."— Walter Iooss, 1998

ISBN 1–888001–56–9 © Copyright under universal copyright convention copyright © 1998 by Graphis Inc., New York, NY 10016. Jacket and Book Design Copyright © 1998 by Pedersen Design,141 Lexington Avenue, New York, NY 10016 USA. No part of this book may be reproduced in any form without written permission of the publisher. Printed in Korea by Doosan Dong -A Co., Ltd.

When Walter Iooss was a teenager in East Orange, New Jersey, he couldn't imagine that anything would ever replace the joy and intensity of the stickball games that absorbed his summer days. Four decades have passed, and now Steve Fine, *Sports Illustrated* magazine's director of photography, calls Iooss the foremost sports photographer of his generation, "a fixture in American journalism to a degree I think people who see the cover of *Sports Illustrated* don't know."

They might be forgiven, although Iooss's shots have graced the cover of *Sports Illustrated* over 200 times. Half of those readers weren't even born in 1959 when Walter got his first assignment at the age of 17. He was told to go to Groton, Connecticut to photograph an octogenarian sailor named Archie Chester, a man who had built a boat with no plans. The picture made the back page. Iooss has built his own craft, four-decades long in the making, also with no plans, just an intuitive gift for light and composition, and a restless internal compass that has kept pointing him back to the basics. In the fall of 1997, the compass pointed him east to the dimly-lit ritualistic world of Thailand's kick-boxers. The Thai retreat proved to be what the photographer had hoped: a cleansing passage back through the "three Walters," Steve Fine's short-hand term for Iooss's artistic evolution, an assessment the photographer accepts.

The first Walter is the one who ran along the sidelines, a guerrilla armed with a Nikon focusing short and long lenses with amazing eye-hand coordination, while the old guard sat in the press box with their fixed-focus Graphlex's. He captured action in a way never seen before, and created a new, freer perspective. It was basic journalism but with a difference: extraordinary backgrounds. Iooss realized that while a 1,000 millimeter lens isolated the tennis player, golfer, outfielder, or wide-receiver he was shooting, the right background created the graphics that often clinched the shot.

There was a favorite background he exploited as he morphed into his second, and subsequent, incarnations. Iooss is like Gulley Jimson, the eccentric painter in Joyce Cary's "The Horse's Mouth." He never met a wall, especially a curiously-lit one, he didn't like. "I love walls. If there isn't one there, I bring one with me." The kind of shots taken by the second Walter evolved from the raw black and whites that are downright sweaty, playful—pure sport—to the color-saturated, "posed" action portraits—pure athlete. This Walter began cataloguing walls and other backgrounds in his head, their best light and shadow, and then waited for the right colored uniforms, or action to come their way. They always did.

The second Walter matured with his swimsuit work. Ah, the *Sports Illustrated* swimsuit issues for which the Iooss lens has born fruit, all the riper for the backgrounds. As in the action shots, the portraits of S.I.'s swimsuit issues reveal an uncanny graphic sense and Rembrandt-like reverence for light and shadow. He sought and found more control in his swimsuit photographs, especially in the early days traveling light with only cameras and beautiful women, without the interference of art directors.

In his wildest dreams, the 16-year-old Walter could not have foreseen such a future as he pulled himself from the stickball field for the trips to Manhattan to attend photography classes. The most memorable featured a model—the first naked girl he'd ever seen. The eye approved. The die was cast. Thank you, Walter.

The third Walter began to emerge in 1982 when he was approached by Fuji film. The teaming unleashed an epic, two-and-a-half- year project to photograph Olympic athletes up to and during the 1984 games. This required a traumatic severing of ties with *Sports Illustrated*, "my psyche, my life since I was 16," as he put it. He has since re-upped.

During the period of advertising work that followed Fuji, with its emphasis on portraiture and its opportunities for technical control, the intense essays of individual athletes he'd created at the Olympics played on his mind.

In the fall of 1992, Iooss approached Michael Jordan with the idea of just such an essay. It would contain both historic and artistic value, he told the star Chicago Bull; like the old photos of Elvis; the young Muhammed Ali. Jordan agreed. The results, presented in the following pages, show the god of basketball in full flight and, perhaps more importantly, as an earthling, a human after all, amid the ethereal trappings of the upper-class athlete. Walter's studies of Michael Jordan are classics. More than the sum of their parts of f-stop and shutter speed, they reveal a relationship between artist and athlete, each in top form.

The third Walter drew the essence of sport from superstars like Jordan, Cal Ripkin Jr., and Ken Griffey, Jr., with whom he helped create the books *Rare Air*, *Cal On Cal*, and *Junior*. The athletes he chose were self-made, he says, not the product of hype or conceit, and their strength of character shows. Iooss was able to draw out their individualities and capture them on film.

He's good with people—a trait his wife Eva attributes in part to a natural gregariousness, but also to his school days at multi-cultural East Orange High. His instincts are those of an athlete. He is a gifted one; once a competitive tennis player. (He once even participated in a doubles match with Bjorn Borg.) Surfing grabbed him hard, and he follows the waves with his sons Christian and Bjorn from his home on Eastern Long Island, New York, to the West Indies and the South Pacific. The surreal beauty of the sport and its environment moved Iooss toward abstraction in his photographs and introduced him to another breed of possessed sportsmen whose souls were ripe for capture.

Iooss likes to call himself "a photo-investigator—Sherlock Holmes with an eye." Perhaps it's why he felt a certain anxiety—"I photograph millionaires"—in deciding to go to Thailand. He wanted to rediscover the raw desire of athletes, unadulterated by money or fame, and to document it using a variety of styles. The chiaroscuro black-and-whites from the kickboxing collection place the teenage warriors in the same

smoky ring as the young Ali, and in the same timeless pantheon as the baseball players he loves the most. But he found a connection between the Thai kickboxers and his friend Michael Jordan: the chance "to be free," Walter says, "to go anywhere you want with no media. It's almost like you're welcomed, whereas you're not a welcomed guest necessarily in a lot of locker rooms or fields. They're just tired of you. It's not you personally. They're just tired of you as a group—the media."

Sadly, the jaded spirit, he has found, is photographable.

His longtime colleagues call him "coast-to-coast Iooss," and Eva Iooss calls her husband "a human Fed-Ex package" for his frenetic travel schedule. He now travels, but with discrimination. The big events like the Super Bowl have lost their allure. It's a more contemplative Iooss, a fourth Walter, the human light meter, who's bringing forth the land and waterscapes of extraordinary color and clarity that he began taking in the 1970s.

And, there's a recent urge to make collage, to explore graphic design in another dimension. As with the collage that appears on the previous page, Walter reaches further into the realm of mixed media. At the same time, Walter's color portraits, like some of his track and field photos, and his more recent surfing waterscapes, are nearly pure abstract expressions of form and color.

To hear him talk, a fifth Walter is in the batter's box. He's the one who intends to seek out the kids in remote places who make do with window shutters for surfboards, and sticks for cricket wickets, because that's where the real action is, and has always been.

"It's always been instinct. In the beginning, I never thought about photographs or photography. I'd get an assignment on a Sunday. It was exciting. You'd tell your friends about it. You'd go to the game and see your heroes, because I was still young and these people were still heroes to me. For years, it went that way. Then, this instinct sort of meshed with my athleticism. My dreams of what sport was, the feeling I get from sport. When I was a Little Leaguer putting my uniform on, it was like Superman putting on his cape. Something came over you. For the moment, if you could squint hard enough in the mirror, maybe I was Mickey Mantle. You were transported into another realm. In high school I would always draw athletes and it was always form: legs, arms, the ballet of sport, bodies in beautiful positions. As time developed, I started to take my fantasies and they'd be manifested in photographs of kids first, Little League and kid's basketball, which I played every day. I was a complete addict. Those things I enjoyed so much, I'd try to get into the picture somehow, like a swish. There's a timing of a jump shot. The release. The swishhhhh."

Walter's passion recalls the words of his gifted predecessor, Henri Cartier-Bresson: "To take photographs is to hold one's breath when all faculties converge in the face of fleeing reality....it is putting one's head, one's eye, and one's heart on the same axis."

"The real joy of photography is these moments," says Iooss. "I'm always looking for freedom, the search for the one-on-one. That's when your instincts come out. I've been lucky enough to have people hire me to do that. *Sports Illustrated* never really restricts me. They want me to do what I do. It's the discovery. It's still magic."

It seems the ingredients of the Iooss styles were all there back then in East Orange: the awestruck fan taking Duke Hodges' name to bat, his eye honed by fast-pitched Spaldings until the end glow of summer sun beat against the backstop.

Russell Drumm is senior writer at New York's EAST HAMPTON STAR, and author of IN THE SLICK OF THE CRICKET. His stories have appeared in GRAPHIS and SMITHSONIAN magazines.

A Life's Work

Baseball

Yogi Berra
Fort Lauderdale, Florida
March 1984 *(previous page)*

Reggie Jackson
Yankee Stadium /The Bronx, New York
August 1980

Twins vs. Dodgers
Holman Field /Vero Beach, Florida
March 1982 *(left page)*

Tom Seaver
Al Lopez Field /Tampa, Florida
March 1981 *(this page)*

Tony Gwynn
San Diego, California
September 1993 *(left page, top left)*

Tommy Green
Wrigley Field / Chicago, Illinois
August 1993 *(left page, top right)*

Dave Parker, Grant Jackson
McKechnie Field / Bradenton, Florida
March 1980 *(left page, bottom left)*

Vida Blue
Candlestick Park / San Francisco, Califiornia
May 1978 *(left page, bottom right)*

Ken Griffey, Jr.
Kingdome / Seattle, Washington
April 1996 *(this page)*

Lou Brock
The World Series, Fenway Park / Boston, Massachusetts
October 1967 *(this page)*

Carl Yastremski
Fenway Park / Boston, Massachusetts
August 1979 *(right page, top)*

Alan Trammell
Tiger Stadium / Detroit, Michigan
July 1993 *(right page, bottom)*

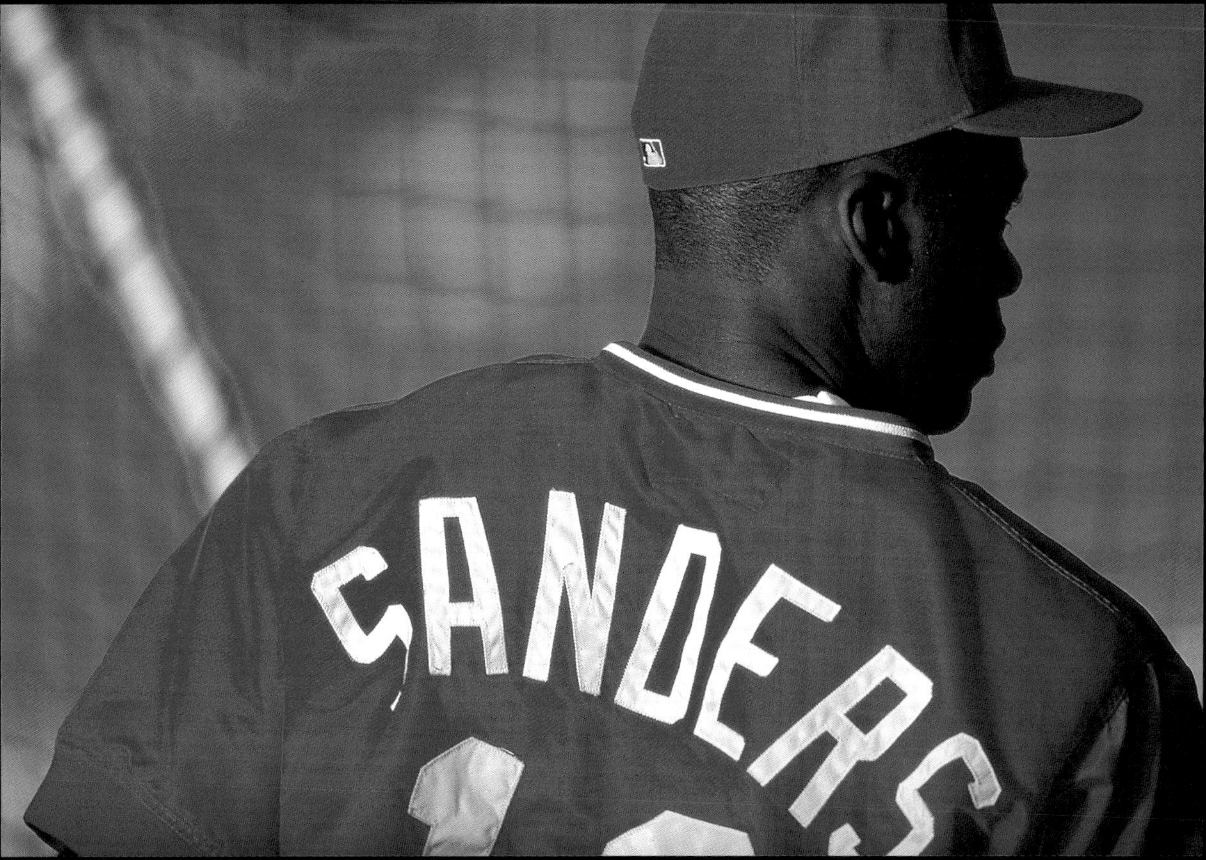
SANDERS

Reggie Sanders
Dodger Stadium / Los Angeles, California
August 1993 *(left page)*

Kevin Mitchell
Candlestick Park / San Francisco, California
August 1993 *(this page)*

Cal Ripkin, Jr.
Al Lang Field / St. Petersburg, Florida
March 1982

Tony Scott, Garry Templeton
Dodger Stadium / Los Angeles, California
June 1979

Edgar Renteria
Miami Beach, Florida
February 1997

Sam McDowell
McKechnie Field / Bradenton, Florida
March 1975 *(left page)*

Ken Griffey, Jr.
Camden Yards / Baltimore, Maryland
August 1996 *(this page)*

Gary Carter
Al Lang Field / St. Petersburg, Florida
March 1980 *(left page)*

John Kruk
Russell Field / Clearwater, Florida
March 1992 *(this page)*

Cal Ripkin Jr.
Ft. Lauderdale, Florida
December 1991 *(following spread)*

Alex Rodriguez
Big Time Studios / Miami Beach, Florida
February 1997 *(this page)*

Ken Griffey, Jr.
Anaheim, California
September 1996 *(right page)*

Cincinnati Reds Bullpen
Wrigley Field / Chicago, Illinois
June 1992

Boston Red Sox
Jack Russell Stadium / Clearwater, Florida
March 1978

Ken Griffey, Jr.
Camden Yards / Baltimore, Maryland
July 1996
September 1989

St. Louis Cardinals Bullpen
Wrigley Field / Chicago, Illinois
September 1989

Basketball

Michael Jordan
Chicago, Illinois
March 1992 *(previous page)*
February 1998 *(this page)*
February 1996 *(right page)*

Michael Jordan
Chicago, Illinois
February 1996 *(this spread)*

Michael Jordan
Coconut Grove, Florida
March 1993 *(following spread)*

Michael Jordan
Lisle, Illinois
July 1987 1988 *(previous spread)*

Phoenix Suns vs. Chicago Bulls
Chicago Stadium / Chicago, Illinois
June 1995 *(left page)*

Michael Jordan
Highland Park, Illinois
March 1998 *(this page)*

Larry Bird
Boston, Massachusetts
April 1989 *(left page)*

Magic Johnson
The Forum / Inglewood, California
February 1996 *(this page)*

Charles Barkley
New York City
September 1993

Charles Barkley
New York City
May 1988

53

Cliff Hagen and Elgin Baylor
Sports Arena / Los Angeles, California
April 1964 *(previous spread, left)*

Wilt Chamberlain, Happy Hairston
The Forum / Los Angeles, California
January 1972 *(previous spread, right)*

Kevin Garnett
New York City
February 1998 *(left page)*

Kobe Bryant
Santa Monica, California
June 1996 *(this page)*

Wes Unseld
Baltimore, Maryland
March 1969 *(previous spread, left)*

Jamaal Mashburn
Lexington, Kentucky
October 1992 *(previous spread, right)*

Wilt Chamberlain
Convention Center / Philadelphia, Pennsylvania
May 1967 *(left page)*

Larry Bird
Boston Garden / Boston, Massachusetts
February 1986 *(this page)*

SEXY PHOTO ROMP

Sports Illustrated

HAWAIIAN Style

Aloha

... CATHY I., HANAUMA BAY ...

... CATHY, WAIKIKI ...

AMBER

... AMBER, DIAMOND HEAD ...

... CATHY, WAIKIKI ...

... CATHY, MAKAPUU/OAHU ...

... SURF, DIAMOND HEAD ...

"SUSHI"

SURF MAKAPUU

DINNER KEOS

- NAME OF THE DAY -
MAKISHA AYESHA WATARU

Nude couple fall off lanai, one dies

Drive-In Condom Shop Vandalized Before Opening

A.M... Kona workout, H₂O. + ENT.
Talked out Friday's Changes...
Story written. Beautiful day...
P.M... Shot around Waikiki... Saw Cathy
at the airport... cloudy as hell day. Caused
P...

Amber Smith
Oahu, Hawaii
November 1992 *(left page)*

Rebecca Romijn
Bermuda
September 1994 *(this page)*

Rachel Hunter
Acapulco, Mexico
December 1988 *(left page)*

Christy Brinkley
La Digue, Seychelles Islands
November 1977 *(this page, top left)*

Ashley Richardson
Turks & Caicos Islands
November 1990 *(top right)*

Elle MacPherson
Malibu, California
December 1993 *(left page)*

Manon Von Gerken
Bermuda
September 1994 *(this page)*

Elle MacPherson
Malibu, California
December 1993 *(this page)*

Vendela
Puerta Vallarta, Mexico
December 1993 *(right page)*

Christy Brinkley
Itapoa Beach, Bahia, Brazil
November 1977 *(left page)*

Roshumba
Ormond Beach, Florida
November 1993 *(this page, following spread)*

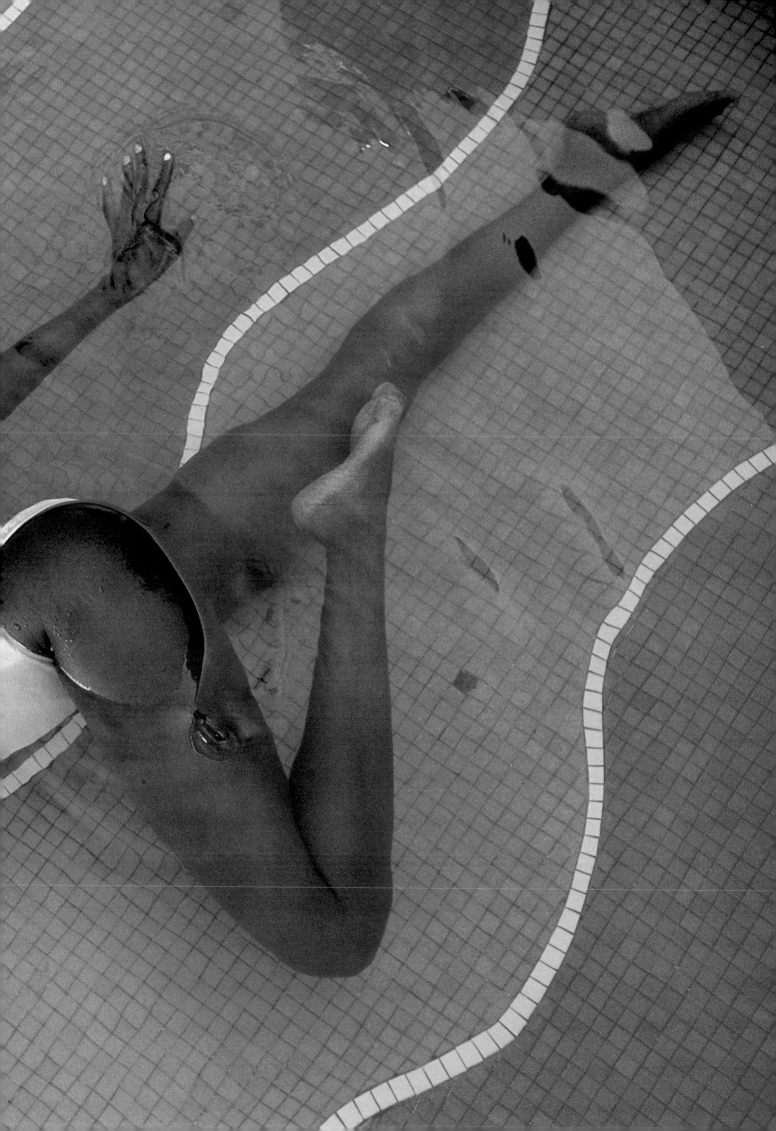

Roshumba
Ormond Beach, Florida
November 1993 *(this page)*

Ashley Richardson, Judith Masco
Providenciales, Turks & Caicos Islands
November 1990 *(right page)*

Erica Peterson
Bimini
December 1989 *(following spread, left)*

Stacey Williams
Miami Beach, Florida
November 1994 *(following spread, right)*

Manon Von Gerken
Bermuda
September 1994

Valaria Mazza
Los Cabos, Mexico
November 1996

85

Valaria Mazza, Tyra Banks
Kleinmond, South Africa
November 1995

Boxing

Muhammed Ali
Berrien Springs, Michigan
September 1996 *(previous page)*

Kickboxer
Lumpinee Stadium, Bangkok, Thailand
April 1997 *(this page)*

Kickboxer
Ratchadumnen Stadium, Bangkok, Thailand
April 1997 *(right page)*

Kickboxer
Ratchadumnen Stadium, Bangkok, Thailand
April 1997 *(this page)*

Kickboxers
Bangkok, Thailand
April 1997 *(right page)*

Kickboxer
Bueng Goom Fairgrounds, Thailand
April 1997 *(following page, left)*

Kickboxer
Lumpinee Stadium, Bangkok, Thailand
April 1997 *(following page, right)*

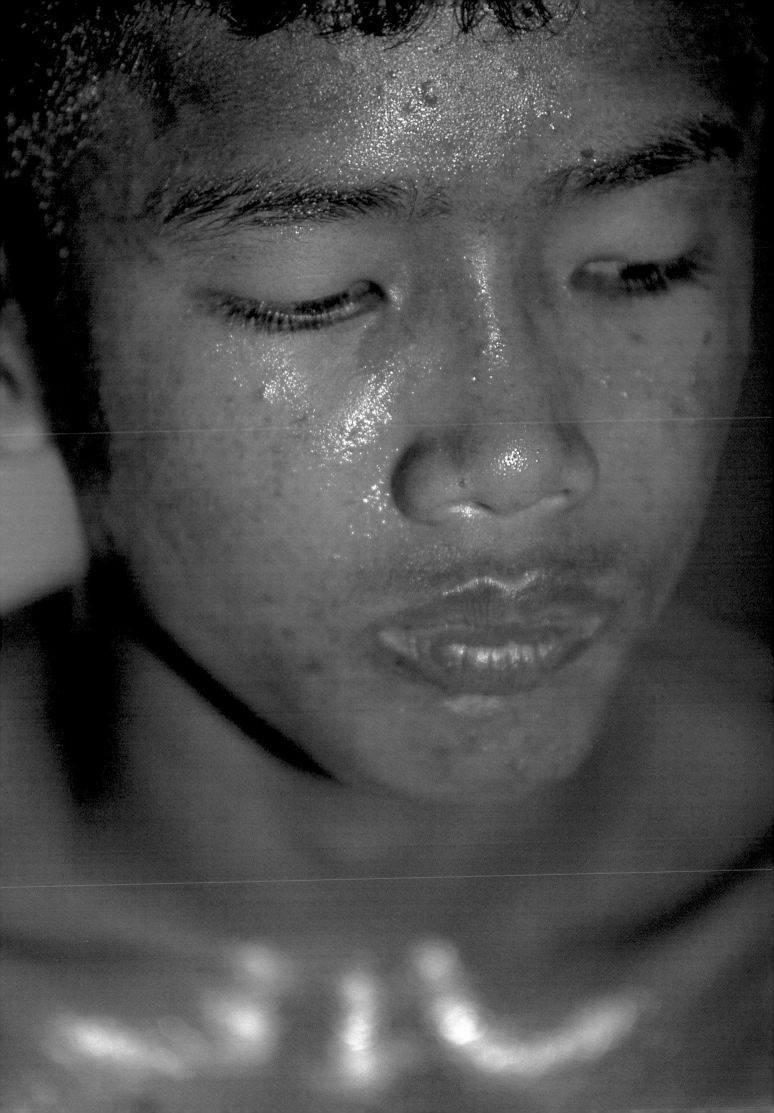

Young kickboxers
Bueng Goom Fairgrounds
Bangkok, Thailand
April 1997 *(this page)*

Young kickboxer
Prasit Boxing Club
Bangkok, Thailand
April 1997 *(right page)*

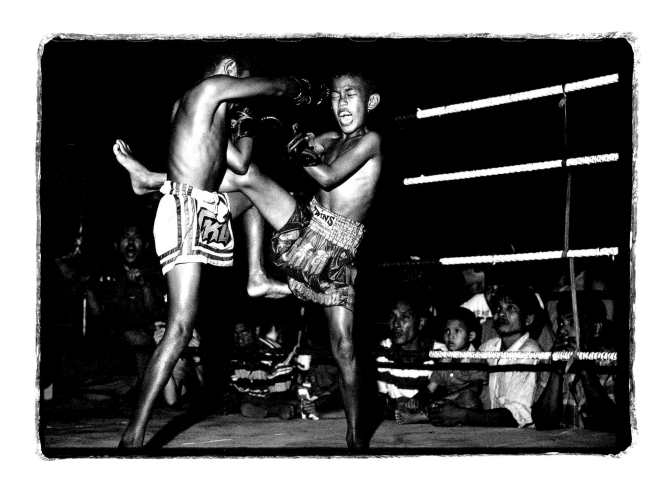

Oscar de la Hoya
Los Angeles, California
March 1995

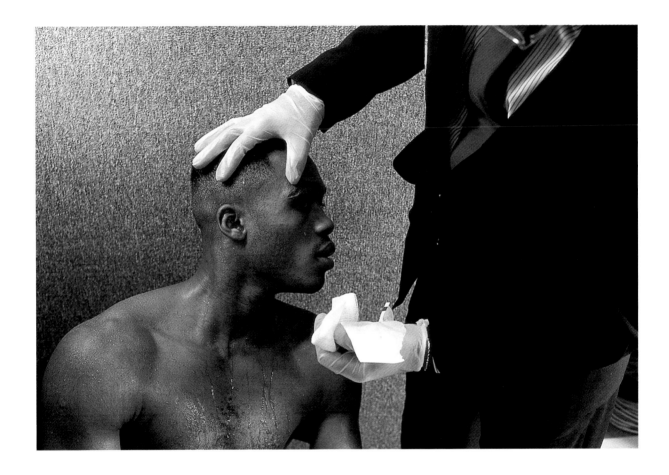

Oscar de la Hoya
Los Angeles, California
March 1995 *(this page)*

"Sugar Ray" Leonard, Thomas "Hitman" Hearns
New York City
February 1989 *(right page)*

Joe Frazier
Philadelphia, Pennsylvania
September 1996 *(left)*

Muhammed Ali
Berrien Springs, Michigan
September 1996 *(right)*

Muhammed Ali
Berrien Springs, Michigan
September 1996

Mark Van Eegan
Memorial Stadium / Baltimore, Maryland
December 1977 *(left page)*

Jack Tatum, John Matusak
Oakland, California
December 1979 *(this page)*

Pittsburgh Steelers vs. New York Giants collage,
Yankee Stadium /The Bronx, New York
December 1962 *(this page)*

Mike "The Bear" Taliferro
Los Angeles, California
May 1995 *(right page)*

Jerry Rice
Los Angeles, California
May 1995

Alvin Harper, Michael Irvin, Dallas Cowboys
Pasadena, California
January 1993

Oakland Raider
Santa Rosa, California
July 1984 *(this page)*

Eddie George
Santa Monica, California
August 1997 *(right page)*

John Elway
Denver, Colorado
January 1998 *(left page)*

Joe Montana
San Francisco, California
October 1991 *(this page top)*

Woody Bennett and the Miami Dolphins
Orange Bowl / Miami Beach, Florida
November 1985 *(this page bottom)*

Keyshawn Johnson
Santa Monica, California
August 1997 *(this page)*

Billy Bates
Texas Stadium / Irving, Texas
December 1994 *(right page)*

Landscape

TAHAA
...MOTU VAHINE...

29th MARCH

...TATU TABU...
ANCIENT POLYNESIAN
TATOOED NATIVES VANISHED
FROM THE ISLANDS AROUND
THE TURN OF THE CENTURY.

HINANO
TAHITI
BIÈRE DE LUXE · BRASSÉE PAR/BREWED BY BRASSERIE DE TAHITI S.A. BP 597 PAPEETE · BP 005 101
ACC./VOL. 4.9% · DLUO 27.02.96 A ‹USED BY›

...I. MOOREA. ARRIVE IN RAIATEA. PICKED UP BY BOAT AND HEAD TOWARDS
VAHINE IS. A.K.A. MOTU TOUVAHINE. AN ISLAND OFF THE N.E. COAST OF
TAHAA. WE ARE THE ONLY GUESTS AT THE HOTEL, WHICH HAS 10 ROOMS
AND OCCUPIES AN ISLAND WITH NO INHABITANTS. WE ARE LIKE SIGNS
FAMILY ROBINSON....

...THE HOTEL HAS FOUR WORKERS LED BY CHARLOTTE ISAUTIER.
BUT THE SOUL OF THE ISLAND IS PAOLO, A PORTAGOSE WITH GREAT
PERSONALITY AND JACK OF ALL TRADES. HE'S JOINED BY IS WIFE
...

VAHINE ISLAND
Private Island Resort

FRENCH POLYNESIA.

Trident Hotel
Port Antonio, Jamaica
February 1989 *(opener)*

Diary spread from French Polynesia
Re-photographed in the Bronx, New York
(previous spread)

St. Maarten
October 1993 *(left page)*

Lovers Beach
Cabo San Lucas, Mexico
November 1996 *(this page)*

Elbow Key, Bahamas
August 1988

Kalalau Beach, Kaui, Hawaii
August 1974

"Lunar Nude," Eva Iooss
Honapu Beach, Kauai, Hawaii
July 1973 *(this page)*

Vahine Island, Raiatea, French Polynesia
December 1996 *(right page)*

Ice

Michelle Kwan
New York City
August 1997

141

Wayne Gretsky
Los Angeles, California
February 1991 *(right page)*

Josh Thompson
Biathlon Training
November 1987 *(next spread)*

Soccer

Michelle Akers
Miami, Florida
February 1990 *(this page)*

Kluivert
Milan, Italy
October 1997 *(right page, top)*

Pro Soccer player
Ft. Lauderdale, Florida
May 1990 *(right page, bottom)*

Surfing

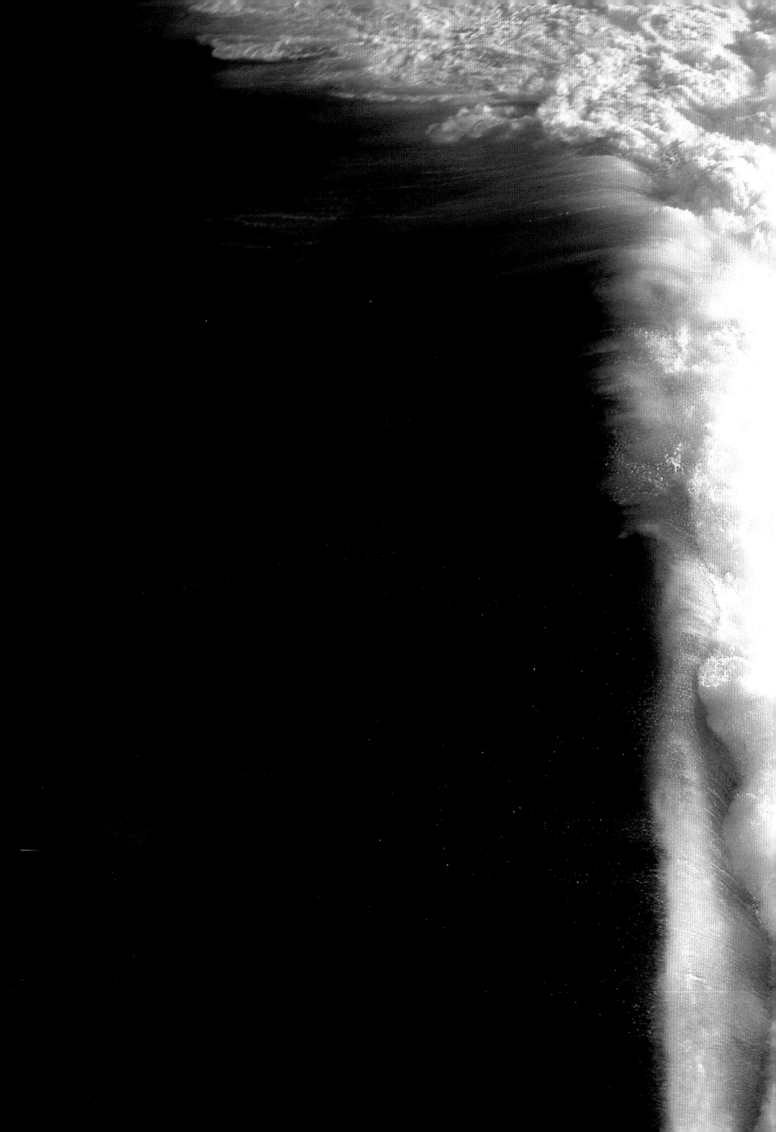

Laird Hamilton
Oahu, Hawaii
January 1995 *(opener)*

Hanalei Bay, Kauai, Hawaii
February 1976 *(previous spread)*

Hanalei Bay, Kauai, Hawaii
February 1976 *(left page)*

Brian Pacheco
Waikiki, Oahu, Hawaii
August 1989 *(this page)*

Kelly Slater
Sebastian Inlet, Florida
October 1990

Na Pali Coast, Kauai, Hawaii
August 1992 *(previous page, left)*

Danny Kim
Sandy Beach, Oahu, Hawaii
August 1990 *(previous page, right)*

Hanalei Bay, Kauai, Hawaii
February 1976 *(this page)*

Kelly Slater
Santa Monica, California
February 1995 *(right page)*

The Pipeline, North Shore, Oahu, Hawaii
January 1990

Kelly Slater
Sebastian Inlet, Florida
October 1990

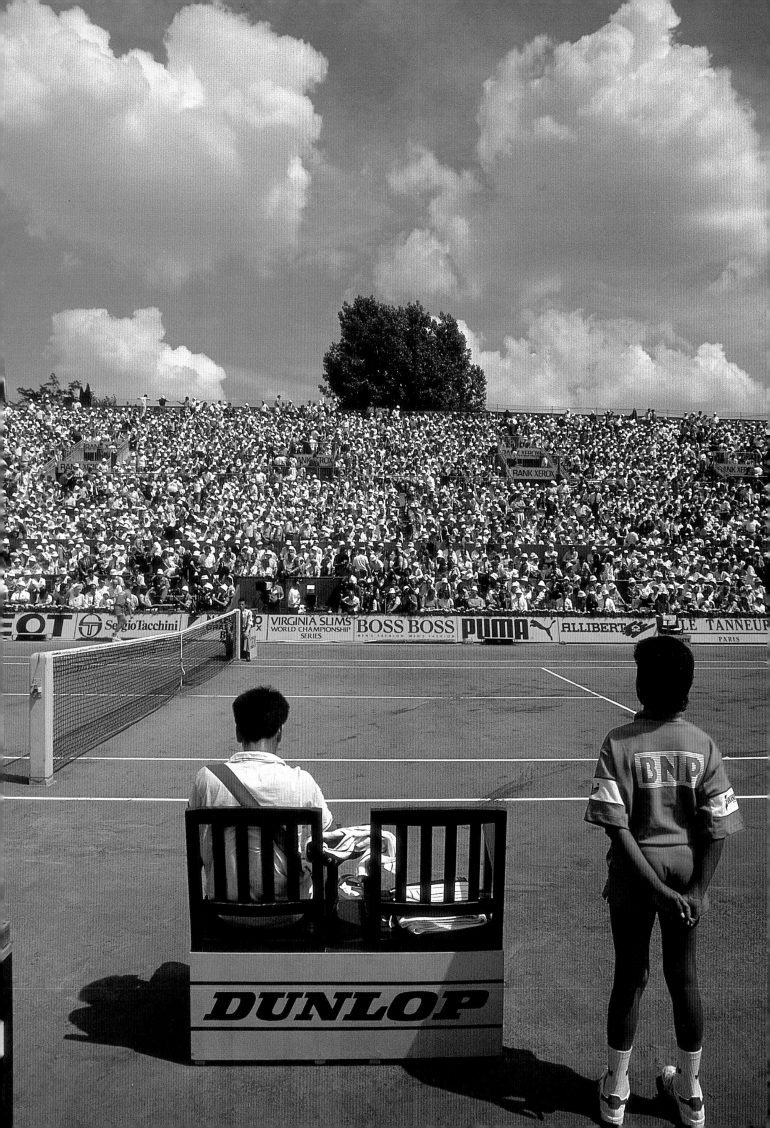

Tennis

Chris Evert Lloyd
U.S. Open / Flushing Meadow, New York
September 1981

Track & Field

Carl Lewis
Houston, Texas
May 1988 *(previous page)*
September 1991 *(this page)*
May 1988 *(right page)*

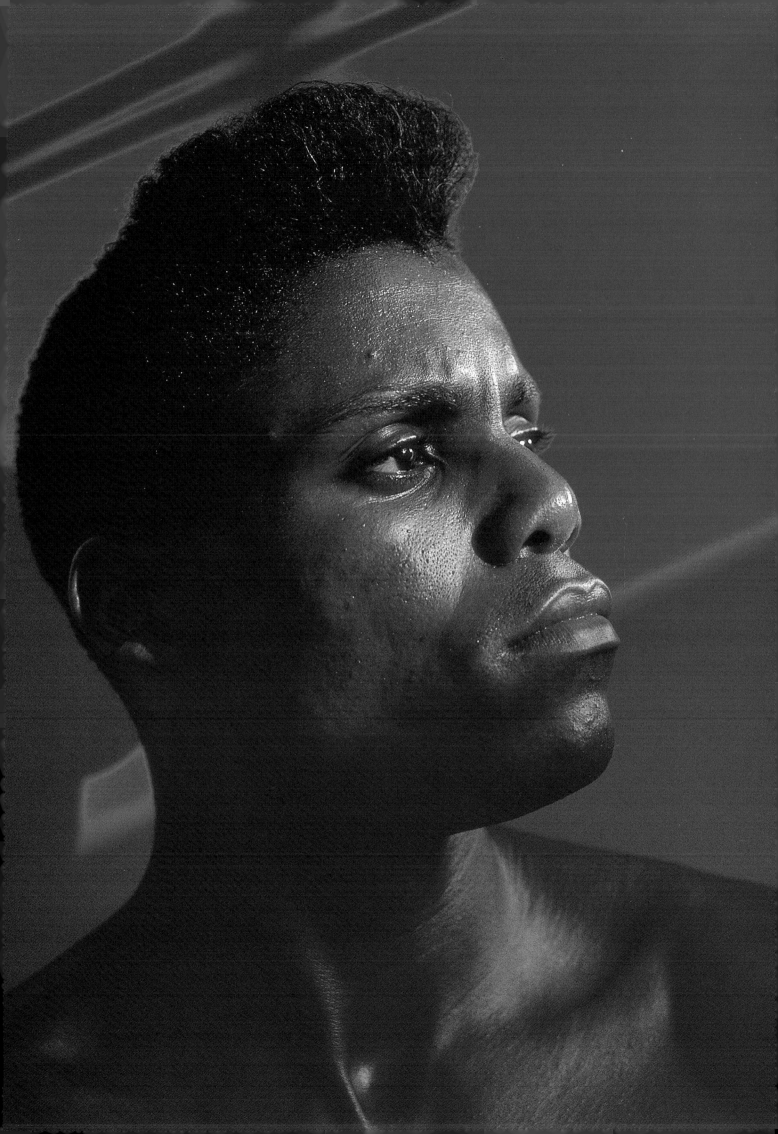

Carl Lewis
Houston, Texas
September 1991 *(this page)*

Gail Devers
University of California Los Angeles / Los Angeles, California
March 1996 *(right page)*

Evelyn Ashford
Indianapolis, Indiana
June 1983 *(left page)*

Jackie Joyner
Los Angeles, California
May 1991 *(this page)*

Calvin Smith
Tuscaloosa, Alabama
October 1983

Edwin Moses
Irvine, California
June 1991

Sam Matatae
Auburn, Alabama
March 1992 *(previous spread, top left, top right)*

Mike Powell
Mount Sac College, California
April 1991 *(previous spread, bottom left)*

Edwin Moses
Huntington Beach, California
November 1983 *(previous spread, bottom right)*

Donovan Bailey
Austin, Texas
March 1996 *(left page)*

Steeplechase
1984 Olympics / Los Angeles Memorial Coliseum
Los Angeles, California *(this page)*

Water

Greg Louganis
Mission Viejo, California
February 1984 *(previous page)*

Swimmers
East Germany
June 1976 *(this page)*

Cloud Diver
Boca Raton, Florida
June 1990 *(right page)*

196

MISSION BAY MAKOS

Todd Torres
Olympic Games / Atlanta, Georgia
August 1996

203

Diver
Olympic Trials / Indianapolis, IN
May 1984

Julia Cruz
Ft. Lauderdale, Florida
January 1994

Paul Barton
Melbourne, Florida
February 1992

Various

Nicole Uphoff
Mainz, Germany
January 1992 *(previous page)*

Kamala, The Ugandan Giant
New Haven, Connecticut
April 1985 *(this page)*

The Alaskans
New Haven, Connecticut
April 1985 *(right page)*

211

211

Captions

front cover: Mike "The Bear" Taliferro, Los Angeles, California, May 1995.

back cover: Elle MacPherson, Malibu, California, December 1993.

Page 2: Mike Powell, New York City, March 1992. Taken at the Polaroid studio. A 20x24-inch Polaroid camera. Film comes in a huge roll, you roll it into the camera. A technician sets it up, shows you the backgrounds you can use. He focuses it. You say, "A little higher, a little to the left." The only thing you do is set the light where you want it.

Page 4: Michael Jordan, Mayfair Hotel, Coconut Grove, Florida, April 1995. Ah, Michael, what can I say? My favorite athlete that I've ever photographed, the most photogenic, certainly the most dominant in my life, since I missed out on Ali. With the beautiful wall, and the shape of his head we came up with one good picture, one of my favorites of Michael.

Page 6: The spiritual headquarters of "Team Iooss:" The house in Montauk, New York.

Page 7: The Iooss team in Tobago taken by Allan Weisbecker, December 1994.

Page 7: Me surfing solo at a point break, the dream of every surfer, near a small town in Mexico, December 1993.

Page 7: Diary spread of Tahiti, re-photographed in Tobago, re-photographed again in Montauk. The layered look of the diary.

Page 8: Team Iooss in our favorite place in the world, French Polynesia in January 1997. Also the place where we hope to celebrate the new millennium. Who knows, we may wind up in Montauk. They're both favorites.

Baseball
Page 10: Yogi Berra, Ft. Lauderdale, Florida, March 1984. This ran on the cover of Sports Illustrated. "Yogi's Back," it read. Not only was his back facing the camera, but he was back from retirement. Problem was, he moved like a butterfly. He'd move when I'd get into position. I'd get set, and he'd take flight again. I was trailing him all day.

Page 12, 13: Reggie Jackson and Goose Gossage, Yankee Stadium, the Bronx, New York, August 1980. We're in a small, closet-like room adjacent to the clubhouse. I just bounced a strobe off one wall and used a 8x10 camera with Polaroid film. I made a few test shots, went into the clubhouse and tried to induce the stars to pose: Jackson, Gossage, Gidrey. Knowing they were going to get a Polaroid, they came. Reggie, of course, was no problem. He loved the camera.

Page 14: Twins vs. Dodgers, Holman Field, Vero Beach, Florida, March 1982. Spring training's the best time of year for baseball. It brings back the historical roots of the game: much quieter, a slower pace, fans and athletes are very close. There are times when the fans actually sit on the field to watch the game, almost like a sandlot game.

Page 15: Tom Seaver, Al Lopez Field, Tampa, Florida, March 1981. At the end of the day in spring training. Seaver was running wind sprints in the outfield by the wall. I saw the foul pole, and the 342, and the pyramid. I asked Seaver to pose because he was the only one I knew who was running laps and I figured he would pose for me. He was a player that would always do something to help you, and the only player I ever knew who actually asked you questions about your life.

Page 16: Tony Gwynn, San Diego, California, September 1993. I was working for Upper Deck trading cards and I was free to shoot a group of players any way I felt was best. I just showed up. Tony said, I can't do it now, how about in two weeks? I said I wouldn't be available. He said, What about three weeks? I said, Why don't we try this: if you want to pose later, I'll be ready for you in the dugout when you come out. He came out and said, I'm ready. It was 15 minutes before game time and the players were putting on their game face, getting real serious. This is their time, usually you don't bother them. He just posed, and stared right into the camera. Ready to play.

Page 16: Tommy Green, Wrigley Field, Chicago, Illinois, August 1993. His face always brings back to me the players of the 20s and 30s, the "Gashouse Gang," the old, gritty, dirty players. This was after batting practice where he was sweating. He must have just pitched batting practice.

Page 16: Dave Parker and Grant Jackson, McKechnie Field, Bradenton, Florida, March 1980. I did a story with the Pirates for a couple years on and off. I was friendly with the team and had great access. Here's a case using a 35mm lens when I was right close to him. They didn't care they were smoking. But later, when this picture ran, Parker was livid. He was warning everyone in spring training that he was going to kill me. Parker was 6'6" and 250 pounds, known as the "Cobra." So I didn't see him for two years, but finally I showed up at spring training. He railed on me, screaming in the batting cage in front of about 20 people: "Never trust this man, never pose for this man." He couldn't have said a worse thing. Trust is everything in this business. When he said that, he killed me. Later on we became friends again.

Page 16: Vida Blue, Candlestick Park, San Francisco, California, May 1978.

Page 17: Ken Griffey Jr., King Dome, Seattle, Washington, April 1996. The King Dome is one of the most hideous baseball parks in America. When you walk in, it's just green light. The fluorescent lights from the ceiling and off the green Astro Turf cast an eerie green on the gray walls, a depressing look. The beauty is, you can climb up on the roof.

Page 18: Lou Brock, Fenway Park, Boston, Massachusetts, October 1967 The World Series, St. Louis vs. Boston. In the background, you can see Kurt Flood falling, trying to scamper back to first base.

Page 19: Carl Yastremski, Fenway Park, Boston, Massachusets, August 1979. Barehanding a grounder. It looks like he's going to toss it to the pitcher covering the bag. In those days, photographers used to work in a

well. It would fill with water when it rained, but you could actually lay your lens on the ground.

Page 19: Alan Trammel, Tiger Stadium, Detroit, Michigan, July 1993. It's one of those you-never-think-you're-going-to-take-again pictures. Trammel was leading off second base in sunlight, beautiful, late light in Tiger Stadium. He took off to steal third. When he hit third base he was in the shade, so I had the roll cut in half and processed; the sunlit roll at a certain exposure, and pushing the remainder two stops, because I knew I had dead solid focus.

Page 20: Reggie Sanders, Dodger Stadium, Los Angeles, California, August 1993.

Page 21: I love the composition of striped grass, how they mow the grass going one way, come back in the opposite direction and cut against the grain. So the shot of Kevin Mitchell at Candlestick was shot specifically with that in mind. I just sat in the stands and waited for something to happen in the outfield. I was shooting all around the batting cages. In Dodger stadium, there are three different sections you can photograph from before the fans come in. As the light changes, you get all these different colors. I had tried on four different occasions to get this picture with the palm trees over a period of about fifteen years. This was the day I finally got it. You have to be there at the right time of the year; can't be there too late or too early. It only takes place in the first two innings. I also used a magenta filter which cleaned up the green on the field and gave the sky the perfect hue.

Page 22: Cal Ripkin Jr., Aclane Field, St.Petersburg, Florida, March 1982. In the dugout. I remember I approached Ripkin to shoot him. I remember he took out a notebook to see what his schedule was. He said, I'm free Thursday, how about that. I said, That's fine. I'd never seen an athlete take out a book. Usually you arrive, they don't, and they say, later, What appointment?

Page 23: Tony Scott and Garry Templeton, Dodger Stadium, Los Angeles, California, June 1979. Here's another shot I saw on a trip preceding this shoot. Late light during batting practice was hitting the dugout wall—robin's egg shell blue. The Phillies were there, their uniforms almost the same but darker. I was shooting around, intrigued with this. Then I remembered the St. Louis uniforms and looked at the schedule. When St. Louis came in, I went back to L.A. and waited. Not only the beauty of the matching blues, but the red of the caps gave it that Caribbean feeling.

Page 24, 25: Alex Rodriguez and Edgar Renteria, Miami Beach, Florida, February 1997. On a Miami rooftop. A story for Sports Illustrated about new, young shortstops creating a stir. This was taken on 4x5 Polaroid film.

Page 26: Sam McDowell, McKechnie Field, Bradenton, Florida, August 1996. Pre-game warm-up.

Page 27: Ken Griffey Jr., Camden Yards, Baltimore, Maryland, August 1996. This was a staged-shot where Griffey accused me of never treating any of the super models this way. "You never made one of them jump up a wall twenty times."

Page 28, 29: Gary Carter at Al Lang Field, St. Petersburg, Florida, March 1980, and John Kruk at Russell Field, Clearwater, Florida, March 1992. Happy-go-lucky Carter, and the very moody, temperamental John Kruk. I was sent down to photograph Kruk for *Philadelphia* magazine. The first time he was sick. The second time, injured. The third time, his P.R. guy said, He doesn't want to do this. I'll bring you in, but you're on your own. Kruk said, I'm not getting dressed. I said, Fine. He said, I'll put on my shirt, but not my hat. I said fine, do anything you want. Okay, he said, I'll bring my hat. So we do the shot. I said, I want you to look intense. That wasn't very hard for John Kruk.

Page 30: Cal Ripkin Jr., Ft. Lauderdale, Florida, December 1991. This was taken on a story for S.I. called "Living Legends." Cal was the last to be added to this group of 10 athletes who were arguably the best athletes to ever play their positions in track and field, tennis, golf, etc. He flew from Baltimore to Ft. Lauderdale where I had set a big, white wall in the stadium and shot from a very low angle in the dugout. We hit fungos at him, and had a minor leaguer throw balls at him at different levels. It was warm down there and when Cal was finished, he was going to get on a plane and go back to Baltimore. Unfortunately, they had turned off all the water in the stadium so Cal flew back with a mighty funk.

Page 32: Alex Rodreguez, Miami Beach, February 1997. The modern-day ballplayer on the rooftop in Miami Beach. A twilight sky, white walls, a fisheye, and a big flash.

Page 33: Ken Griffey, Jr. Anaheim, California September 1996. I worked on a book with Jr. from March through September. You're always thinking "cover"—I was thinking it from the very first day that we shot in Arizona for spring training. It's the hardest picture to get. This was the last day I shot Jr. Not only was it the last day I shot him for the book, but this was one of the last two frames. Once again, 4x5 Polaroid in the bullpen at Anaheim. The shot. The cover.

Page 34: Cincinnati Reds Bullpen, Wrigley Field, Chicago, Illinois, June 1992. You go there in June for the best late-day light, until about 8:30. You take a strobe, send your assistant up in back, get with a wide-angle lens, and hang over the bullpen.

Page 34: Jack Russell Stadium, Clearwater, Florida, March 1978. The magic in spring training that takes place occasionally. Photographers don't like to go to night games—the lights are bad. Who wants to stay up all night photographing a spring training game? But they miss out on one great thing. Batting practice starts at about five so you get this wonderful light. And the game starts with absolute perfect balance between the lights hitting the field and the twilight being the same exposure as the field. You get this perfect balance. Here's the full moon rising over the stadium with the Boston Red Sox taking batting practice.

Page 35: Ken Griffey Jr., Camden Yards, Baltimore, Maryland, July 1996. Here's another case where I brought a strobe into effect at twilight, actually a small soft box—not done too often in baseball during a game.

Page 35: St. Louis Cardinals Bullpen, Wrigley Field, Chicago, Illinois, September 1989.

Basketball

My access to Michael is such an important part of what has happened: the relationship we've developed over 10 or 11 years now, and of course *Rare Air*. March and April of '98 was as enjoyable a period as I've ever spent with a team in my life. At this stage in my career I see the distant horizons about a lot of things, whereas in your 40's you never thought about distant horizons. Now I see my career and I see his career. I see what these pictures are going to mean in 20 years, just as Ali's pictures have come back as statements 20 years later. The '90s will be a phenomenal era to look back at: a fantastic economy, no inflation, the Viagra kid as president, the bull run in the market, and you've got the Chicago Bulls. I see that now, and I see that I'm lucky to get a second chance at doing something I love. I've spoken about this to Michael. We both love what we do. I think we both respect each other's passions. He knows I'm very passionate about what I do, and I respect his passion as a basketball player. Here's a man who could circumvent all the rules of life and no one would say anything to him. Michael doesn't play that game. He plays by the rules of honesty, commitment, what's right and wrong, gut feelings. I'm amazed by him. His background with his family is so good. He's got such a straight point of view of how to live life and do it right. That's what I respect about him the most.

Page 36: Michael Jordan, Chicago, Illinois, March 1992. This was taken on a Gatorade shoot and all Michael did was float in front of a background. Of course everything he does looks balletic. You'll notice the shoes are running shoes. The Gatorade people forgot to bring basketball shoes so none of these pictures were ever used.

Page 38: Michael Jordan, Chicago, Illinois, February 1988. Michael's famous slam dunk victory in Chicago. The peak of his Airness. He drove from one end of the court leaped from the foul line slammed the ball and landed in my lap because I was lying right under the basket.

Page 39: Michael Jordan, Coconut Grove, Florida, March 1993. An advertising shoot, all black and white, but I had a little colored gel on the strobe which they didn't realize. The background was red, which would go dark for the black and white, so I snuck this roll of color in.

Page 40: Michael Jordan, Chicago, Illinois, February 1996. Another roll of sneaky color of Michael just standing there flipping the ball. An off moment that often makes the best pictures.

Page 41: The portrait is from the same black and white shoot in '96. The collage is a group of my basketball favorites from the '60s through the '90s.

Page 42: Michael Jordan, Coconut Grove, Florida, March 1993. Michael in bed at the Mayfair Hotel. I was to meet Michael after practice that day at noon in his room. I knocked on his door. He let me in, didn't say hello, turned his back, walked to his bed and laid down, exhausted. He said he didn't sleep that night, so I asked if I could open the curtains just a bit so I could get some light. He just lay there with his clicker. That clicker for the TV was always by his side. He kept nodding in and out of consciousness. I just took a roll and left.

Page 44: Michael Jordan, Lisle, Illinois, July 1987. The blue dunk, taken at a camp he runs for children. Painted a section of parking lot red and another section blue. And then we brought in an official N.B.A. basket and rolled that into position. The beauty of a movable basket is, I can place it and get the shadow in the exact position. The shadow was the key element to add a third dimension. We thought the blue looked best against his red uniform. Taken with a high-speed camera.

Page 46: Chicago Stadium, June 1995. Taken during the play-offs, Phoenix versus the Bulls. This was just a mix of strobes set up in the arena. That way you get the blur.

Page 47: Michael Jordan, Highland Park, Illinois, March 1998.

Page 48: Magic Johnson, Beverly Hills, California, August 1991. Taken at Magic's house. What I remember most about that shoot was that Magic came out of his house in uniform, all six-foot, nine-inches of him. You talk about an athlete being bigger than life. Magic was bigger than life; tan from being in Hawaii, buff from the weight room. He looked fantastic. A few months later, Magic tested positive for the HIV virus.

Page 49: Michael Jordan, Highland Park, Illinois, March 1998. M.J. against a green and red background in his home for the cover of his retirement book. Using the red and the green was something I'd seen in a renaissance painting of a cardinal in a red shawl, against a green background.

Page 50: Larry Bird, Boston, Massachusetts 1989. This was taken when he was injured with a bad back. I had so much time with Larry, knowing he wasn't playing. This was for the dust jacket of his book, so it meant something to him. GQ asked me once to photograph him. I approached Larry and asked for 5 minutes. He said, No, no, no. I said, Four minutes on a stop watch. He said, No. Two minutes on a stop watch, one minute on a watch, and if I'm not set up in time, you can leave. He still wouldn't pose. Here's an example of an athlete slowed down by an injury and having the time to pose and to be very reflective.

Page 51: Magic Johnson, The Forum, Inglewood, California, February 1996. This was taken when Magic came back from his retirement due to the HIV virus. Magic—his nickname is not just from his ability to play, but his magical personality. One of the most compelling athletes I've every photographed. Here he is just leaping and laughing with that incredible smile, for the cover of *Time* magazine.

Page 52: Charles Barkley, New York City, September 1993. He's in a limo, in a picture taken for *People* magazine. Barkley is guy who I'd never really appreciated as a personality in basketball. I liked the way he played, but I always hated his attitude on the court. But once again, as you so often find out, a person's court demeanor or field demeanor, and his personal demeanor are different things. He's an amusing, personable guy.

Page 53: Charles Barkley, New York City, May 1988. A Nike shoot.

Page 54: Cliff Hagen and Elgin Baylor, Sports Arena, Los Angeles, April 1964. Elgin Baylor was famous for his "leapin' leaners," one of the great players of his generation and basically the predecessor to Dr. J, and from Dr. J, to Michael.

Page 55: Wilt Chamberlain, Happy Hairston, The Forum, Los Angeles, January 1972. The Stilt and Happy. Just a rebound shot.

Page 56: Kevin Garnett, New York City, February 1998. The 120-million-dollar man—his salary over a period of years. One frame of a sepia Polaroid. I was most struck by that beautiful cheekbone and long neck of his. He almost looks Ethiopian. A very interesting guy to photograph.

Page 57: Kobe Bryant, Santa Monica, California, June 1996. The alleged future of the NBA, a fantastic young man. Taken on a trampoline for Adidas. He just had an ability to fly through the air.

Page 58: Wes Unseld, Baltimore, Maryland, March 1969. One of my early portraits to appear on the cover of S.I. Wes was a big, huge man about 6'10," 270 pounds, an immovable object on the court.

Page 59: Jamaal Mashburn, Lexington, Kentucky, October 1992. Taken at the University of Kentucky. I wanted to give him the classic college look with the "K" letter sweater. S.I. hated this picture. It never ran.

Page 60: Wilt Chamberlain, Convention Center, Philadelphia, Pennsylvania, May 1967. A color shot I always loved. But going through the S.I. files one day I found an 8 x 10 black-and-white they'd made from the color, and it just blew away the color shot. The black and white gave it a timelessness. It's Wilt against his nemesis, the Celtics. The collage was completed Montauk in '98.

Page 61: Larry Bird, Boston Garden, Boston, Massachusetts, February 1986. Dedicated. He was always practicing always shooting. The Garden with the banners for the Bruins championships hanging from the rafters.

Beauty
You know, strangely enough, no matter what you have done over the years at *Sports Illustrated* over the years—the covers, the stories—it really comes down to one question: Have you done the swimsuit issue? It's one of the most cherished assignments, and probably the best single assignment for an American photographer, any photographer. Every day you wake up with the chance to take a truly great shot.

Page 62: Rachel Hunter, Acapulco, Mexico, December 1988. Taken on a patio outside my room at the Las Brisa Hotel. Francois, the makeup guy, had a stand fan to blow her hair. As the light dropped in the Pacific I took this shot.

Page 64: Hawaiian diary spread from a November, '92 swimsuit issue. Re-shot at Makapuu Beach, Oahu in Dec. of '93.

Page 65: Valeria Mazza, Arnistan, South Africa, November 1995.

Page 66: Amber Smith, Oahu, Hawaii, November 1992. On her patio, which we lit with a hot light to give it that old glamour of the '40s.

Page 67: Rebecca Romijn, Bermuda, September 1994.

Page 68: Paulina Porizkova, Montego Bay, Jamaica, November 1982. The young, 17-year-old future star, in her first swimsuit issue in Jamaica. When she arrived at the exclusive Half-moon Bay Club, she wore a t-shirt, hand-written, that said, "Too Drunk to Fuck." It was a very stodgy hotel. Jule Campbell, the swimsuit editor, was begging, Please Walter, you've got to get her to change that t-shirt. So I said, You can wear that t-shirt for the rest of your life Paulina, but please, while you're down here with Jule. don't wear it again. She was beautiful from every angle.

Page 69: Cheryl Tiegs, Port Antonio, Jamaica, November 1982.

Page 70: Rachel Hunter, Acapulco, Mexico, December 1988. A feisty woman with a bawdy sense of humor.

Page 71: Christy Brinkley, La Digue, the Seychelles Islands, November 1977.
La Digue, known for its eroded granite rocks.

Page 71: Ashley Richardson, Turks and Caicos Islands, November 1990. One of my favorite models for her movements. She could move and come up with concepts for motion like few models can. She was totally free-spirited.

Page 71: Monique Moura de Caravalito-Manaus, Brazil, November 1978. A very small model, a local Brazilian girl. She couldn't have been more than 5'2". We took her to this pond with a dugout canoe, which was extremely shaky. I was terrified about falling into this pond, and so was she. The water had evaporated, and it was as if the first crawling creature on the planet must have come from this swamp. It made the Hudson look like the Caribbean. We took this at noon and got out of there.

Page 71: Paulina Porizkova, Montego Bay, Jamaica, November 1982.

Page 72: Elle MacPherson, Malibu, California December 1993. The legendary Elle on a pool deck. Elle always reminds me of Michael Jordan in a strange way because their bodies are so wonderful: broad shoulders, long arms, long legs. It's almost impossible to take a bad picture of either one. They always look good. The difference is that Michael is very secure in the way he looks. Elle was insecure, surprisingly.

Page 73: Manon Von Gerken, Bermuda, September 1994. One of my favorites, taken on a horrible day. We'd set up on two rocks with a big ring light and a big six-by-seven camera and just kept shooting. One of my favorite pictures I've ever taken over the swimsuit years.

Page 74: Elle MacPherson, Malibu, California December 1993. Malibu bound at twilight.

Page 75: Vendela, Puerta Vallarta, Mexico, December 1993. The perfectly-defined Vendela. Not too big anywhere, and not too small anywhere.

Page 76: Christy Brinkley, Brazil, November 1977. This was the first morning of the Brazil shoot. The sun comes up real early, 4:30, they said. We got up at 3. The sun didn't come up until quarter after six. We were ready to take the picture. She's always been one of my favorites: full of energy, great face, great look, phenomenal hair. We used to call her "smokin' Christy Brinkley." She was like a thousand-watt bulb.

Page 77: Roshumba, Ormond Beach, Florida, November 1993. The best hand movements. Beautiful, lyrical hands.

Page 78: Roshumba, Ormond Beach, Florida, November 1993. In the pool. You see her hands there.

Page 80: Roshumba again at Ormond Beach, Florida in '93.

Page 81: Ashley Richardson and Judith Masco, Providenciales, Turks and Caicos, Islands, November 1990. Look at those faces!

Page 82: Erica Peterson, Bimini, December 1989. This was taken on an ad job, and this woman possessed the most beautiful bottom of all time, so I kept posing her on the beach much to the glee of my art director.

Page 83: Stacey Williams, Miami Beach, Florida November 1994. A famous location that used to be called the Spear House, abstractly designed, thus the pose with Stacey taken with a wide angle. One of the favorite S.I. girls.

Page 84: Manon Von Gerken, Bermuda, September 1994. Every day I would ride my bike to get exercise and cleanse the mind. It was also a great way to see locations. I discovered this pool, at the Blue Horizons Motel. On a gray day with no wind we took Manon there. The stylist created this nautilus look for her.

Page 85: Valaria Mazza, Los Cabos, Mexico, November 1996. At the Regina Hotel. Beautiful girl from Argentina and a very futuristic, modern, newly painted hotel.

Page 86: Valaria Mazza and Tyra Banks, Kleinmond, South Africa, November 1995. Here's a case where *Sports Illustrated* picked my single best photograph for the cover. It was also the first swimsuit cover to feature an African-American woman. The shot had all the variables for a good cover: beautiful women, sand, joy, and sun.

Page 87: Valaria Mazza, Kleinmond, South Africa, November 1995.

Boxing
Page 88: Muhammed Ali, Berrien Springs, Michigan, September 1996. The first encounter I ever had with Ali one-on-one. Of course by now his faculties had dimmed a little from Parkinson's so he doesn't have the same fire. I tried everything to get the fire in his eyes—get some spark. So I started talking in racial terms about that big old ugly gorilla Joe Frazier, that big old ape. I didn't know what he'd do, but he started to get that fire again in his eyes, and he started to liven up. Then I'd stop talking. He'd shut his eyes and almost go to sleep, then I'd bring up that big old ugly gorilla Joe Frazier again and he'd start to do it. He still has the magic. It's in his heart, but it doesn't come out in his body anymore.

Page 90: Lumpinee Stadium, Bangkok, Thailand, April 1997. A young kick boxer.

Page 91: Ratchadumnen Stadium, Bangkok, Thailand, April 1997. The essence of sport: pure, untouched, no press, no media, free to roam, free to do what you want. The colors and traditions of the sport are fantastic.

Page 92: Ratchadumnen Stadium, Bangkok, Thailand, April 1997. Before each fight the kickboxer, the "muaythai participant" is seen to a seat in the stadium where he can watch the next match before he goes in. That's where they get their game face on.

Page 93: Bangkok, Thailand, April 1997. A training facility in someone's home. A lot of these facilities are very rural and very small where they get kids from the area to train in a ring under someone's garage roof. I saw these kids lean over the ropes once. The Hasselblad is a kind of slow-acting camera. I had a strobe. The interpreter asked if I wanted them to do it again. This was the picture—the ballet of kickboxing.

Page 94: Bueng Goom Fairgrounds, Thailand, April 1997. The single best day I had in Thailand. A very small fairgrounds, the boxer all greased with his liniment before his fight. Hit with a strobe.

Page 95: Lumpinee Stadium, Bangkok, April 1997. With a strobe, taken in a little tiny stadium. Every boxer has liniment rubbed on him.

Page 96: Bueng Goom Fairgrounds, Thailand, April 1997. The single best night. The fans literally came to edge of the ring to cheer on the young kids who were boxing. The ring was set up in a dirt area where they put plastic around some posts that made a fence to keep non-payers out. It had 12 bulbs over the ring and that was the only light illuminating the area. It was like a dungeon, but full of electricity and wonderful pictures. I tried to light them like the old boxing pictures. I had my assistant back away from the ring with a strobe and he would just let it loose by radio. Where ever I'd shoot from, he'd be somewhere else. I would just move him to get angles with the light.

Page 97: Prasit Boxing Club, Bangkok, April 1997. Taken at the most vile of all the Thai facilities. It was under an eight-lane expressway surrounded by six lanes of surface roads. Anyone who knows Asia knows the belching, colossal fumes and traffic that suffocate the towns. These kids train 7 hours a day. Taken in front of a black board training schedule with a little flash that I held beneath his chin.

Page 98: Oscar de la Hoya, Los Angeles, California, March 1995. This was taken for a men's calendar for S.I. The location was a former prison, so it had some fantastic backgrounds, fantastic walls.

Page 99: Owen McGeachy, Madison Square Garden, December 1997. Taken at a Golden Gloves boxing tournament. He may look like he's lost, but he was the victor in this match.

Page 100: Osca de la Hoya, Los Angeles, California, March 1995. De la Hoya back in the prison. I put a ring light in a fixture on the ceiling and lit the situation with a blue gel.

Page 101: Sugar Ray Leonard and Tommy "hit man" Hearns, New York City, February 1989. Taken for a Caesar's Palace fight poster.

Page 102: Joe Frazier, Philadelphia, Pennsylvania, and Muhammed Ali, Berrien Springs, Michigan, September 1996. Now you can see Ali's face. Joe Frazier was still agitated about Ali and all the detrimental things he said, calling him an ignorant share-cropper, a gorilla: "he's ugly." He started to talk to me about Ali and how much it agitated him: "Why'd he have to say that?" Twenty-five years later, Joe was still burning.

Page 103: Muhammed Ali, Michigan, September 1996. This is at Ali's farm in Michigan. Strangely enough, this day I was thinking what Annie Liebovitz, one my favorite photographers—what would she do in the same situation? I saw this fence and Ali was just riding around on this bike while I was looking for locations. I told him to take his bike by the fence and stand there. I would never have thought of putting Ali on a bike, but it's easier for him to ride than walk at this stage of his life.

Football

Page 104: What Cheer, Iowa, August 1975. I did a story on kids' football. I looked for towns with strange names, like Wink, Texas; West Berlin, Vermont; and What Cheer, Iowa. I went across the country in these rural communities looking for the essence of the sport. and I found these kids and brought them out to this road, which was a beautiful location, and took a picture of them playing touch football.

Page 106: Dick Modzelewski, Green Bay, Wisconsin, January 1966. Of course, this is the way I think football should look. Mud, rain, and misery make beautiful pictures.

Page 107: Collage, completed August 1997. These were originally color shots. I found these black and white contacts I hadn't looked at in years. I thought of putting together, a mayhem and violence collage from the '70s from when all these pictures were taken.

Page 108: Mark Van Eegan, Memorial Stadium, Baltimore, Maryland, December 1977. An S.I. cover. When I looked at the picture before this one, and the one after it, in the motorized sequence, the other two pictures were grossly out of focus and somehow this was perfectly in focus. That's called luck.

Page 109: Jack Tatum and John Matusak, Oakland, California, December 1979. Taken at the Oakland-Alameda coliseum. Tatum was known as the "assassin." He was the defender that broke Daryl Stingly's neck and paralyzed him for life. Matusak, a very good-looking, thespian-type football player, was taking acting lessons and he told me he could project an image, so I told Tatum to look as mean as possible, which was simple, and Matusak was acting like Shakespeare. One of my favorite pictures I've ever taken of football players.

Page 110: Collage, the central shot of Steelers versus Giants, December, 1962. Probably, hands-down, my favorite picture ever, taken at Yankee Stadium. Unfortunately, I haven't been able to match it still 35 years later. The collage was the first I did of Polaroids around one central picture, and they encompass the pros, college, and kid's football.

Page 111: Mike "The Bear" Taliferro, Los Angeles, California, May 1995. We're under a tree in broad daylight to shade my subjects from the light. In this case, one sheet of 4x5 Polaroid film and the Bear. He's a former pro football player, used this particular day as an actor for a Nike shoot.

Page 112: Drew Bledsoe, Los Angeles, May 1995. For Nike.

Page 113: Jerry Rice, Los Angeles, California, May 1995.

Page 114: Cleveland Browns, Municipal Stadium, Cleveland, Ohio, October 1979. Just a wonderful sky.

Page 115: Alvin Harper and Michael Irvin, Pasadena, California, January 1993. Celebrating their Super Bowl 27 victory. The sky is smoky because of all the fireworks, but that's what makes this picture a little more interesting.

Page 116: Unknown Oakland Raider, Santa Rosa, California, July 1984. The Torso. This was a Raider rookie. I was there assigned to cover the Raiders for GQ. Let me tell you, I've worked for S.I. for years, but working for GQ, the players will line up to pose, thinking that they're fashion plates. This guy never made the team.

Page 117: Eddie George, Santa Monica, California, August 1997. Taken for Adidas. As soon as I saw him put a towel over his head I thought of the Rare Air cover. He loved this shot. He said it reminded him of the cover of Rare Air. I told him I'd taken that cover. He was as good-looking as Michael Jordan.

Page 118: John Elway, Denver, Colo., January 1998. Taken the week before the Super Bowl in '98. A sepia Polaroid. I'd never met him before, a very funny and engaging character.

Page 119: Joe Montana, San Francisco, California, October 1991. For S.I.'s Living Legends series. The first time I went to San Francisco, he stood us up, called it off. The second time he was injured, and like Larry Bird, he had time on his hands, but he wanted to leave before sunset and the only time I wanted to do the shot was after sunset, so I bought a six-pack of beer and tried to delay things. We had a Corona, and another Corona, and now he's telling me all kinds of inside secrets about the team, more than I ever wanted to know. Then we went to shoot. He stayed until dark. Good old Joe.

Page 119: Woody Bennett, Orange Bowl, Miami Beach, Florida, November 1985. Access is everything once again. No photographer is allowed behind the bench to shoot. Not only was I behind the bench but had an assistant with a strobe to illuminate it. I'd covered the Miami dolphins all season, so by this point I could do anything I wished.

Page 120: Keyshawn Johnson, Santa Monica, California, August 1997. I'd heard a lot of bad things about Keyshawn before this shoot—being late for shoots, petulant, never smiling, a pain.

We would have a contest before each of these shoots, guessing what time the limo would arrive with the millionaire. But Keyshawn was a joy.

Page 121: Billy Bates, Texas Stadium, Irving, Texas, December 1994. I always loved working in Texas stadium because of the open roof. It's always a compositional force, an interesting background. This was a dark day, a very gray day with drizzle. I illuminated him with strobe and a heavy warming filter and tried to balance out the sky to get some light up there. Everything else would go black. This was pre-game.

Landscape
Page 122: The Trident Hotel, Port Antonio, Jamaica, February 1989.
Pool overlooking the Atlantic.

Page 124: Diary spread from French Polynesia. Re-photographed in the Bronx with all my shells. Two places you normally don't put in the same sentence.

Page 126: St. Maarten, October 1993.
A pool we used for a swimsuit session high above the Caribbean.

Page 127: Lovers Beach, Cabo San Lucas, Mexico, November 1996. One of my favorite beaches in the world for its magnificent rock formations. In this case, I lit it softly with a little, hand flash at twilight to give the rocks some texture and to be able to see the sky in proper exposure.

Page 128: House in Saba Island, November 1984.

Page 129: A sand spit in Elbow Key, Bahamas.

Page 130: Kalalau Beach, Kaui, August 1974. Here's one of these shots you take once in your life and never again. The perfect balance of water and extremely low tide, a very rugged beach with heavy surf often and the contrast between the black rocks, the water, and the deep blue sky.

Page 131: Philippines, February 1987.
A little girl on her patio.

Page 132: Eva Iooss, Honapu Beach, Kauai, July 1973. Eva Iooss, nude in Kauai, looking beautiful. We were dropped by helicopter, which is illegal now. In those days there were no air restrictions. We spent the day on the beach nude. This was the most primal place I've ever been. The next piece of land looking out over the pacific was Alaska, 5,000 miles away. There was a stream there with little fish that would swim straight to you. They had no fear of man. In the background, an enormous cliff that hung slightly over the beach, and a huge dune.

Page 133: Vahine Island, Raiatea, French Polynesia, December 1996. Pathway to heaven. My favorite hotel in the world. We stayed in the front two bungalows. This island has 10 huts, no inhabitants.

Page 134: Cancun, Mexico, November 1972. This was taken during a swimsuit issue for *S.I.* I remember crawling on my hands and knees to get close to these birds with a 400 millimeter

lens. They were facing directly into the wind. At that time, Cancun had no hotels. Within a year it looked like a city.

Page 135: Saba Island, Novemer 1984. This is Hurricane Klaus ripping apart the hotel I stayed in. Shot out the door which had been blown into my room.

Ice
Page 136: Nick Tometz, Butte, Montana, November 1987. This is the starting position for speed skaters, a very elegant pose.

Page 138, 139: Bonnie Blair, Butte, Montana, November 1987. The great Bonnie Blair—and again, gasping for air after practice in those fantastic skin-tight uniforms.

Page 140: Jeremy Roenick, Chicago, Illinois, January 1994. This was for Upper Deck trading cards, taken in the upper deck of the old Chicago Stadium.

Page 141: Michelle Kwan, New York, August 1997. This was for the Good Will Games. I built a platform on the rooftop where we could see the Chrysler Building and the Empire State Building. It was an extremely polluted night so I added filtration to get some color to the sky, and on the platform we put black Plexiglas to get the feeling of ice and reflection. I didn't want any color to draw the eye down to the bottom of the picture. I just wanted Michelle to be the picture and that's how we did it on the rooftop.

Page 142: Wayne Gretzky and Magic Johnson, Los Angeles, December 1989. A rarity to see two of the greats of sport, and even more unusual to see them in sunlight which is how I wanted to do this because Gretsky you always see under the lights on the ice, and magic under the lights on the floor, so I took them on a roof top in Los Angeles.

Page 143: Wayne Gretsky, Los Angeles,February 1991.This was for the Living Legends series. I was on the ice. They were pushing me down the ice trying to get some motion which never really worked, but the angle's nice as he hit slap shots. He's one of the gentlest of all the athletes I ever met. It looks like he'd never body shake anyone. He fixed me breakfast, a very kind, gentle man

Page 144: Josh Thompson, Sun Valley, Idaho, November 1987. Taken for *Life Magazine's* winter olympic preview issue. Biathaletes such as Thompson must crosscountry ski at high speeds and then abrubtly stop to shoot at a target. It's a special skill that takes extreme concentration.

Soccer
Page 146: Zanetti, Milan, Italy, October 1997. Taken for Adidas. It rained all day from the moment I woke up to the moment I went to bed except for the hour and-a-half we shot. That's what gave us the wonderful sky. The clubs are very popular but very secretive. They don't want you to watch anything. Beautiful clubs with cappuccino machines.

Page 148: Hierro, Madrid, Spain, June 1997.

Page 149: Pele, New York City, July 1987. The first time I shot him it was in a

studio in New York City. And once again, like Ali, and Jordan—not only are these athletes fantastic, physically in what they do, but they all had wonderful personalities and great smiles. It takes more than sheer physical ability to be great.

Page 150: Michelle Akers, Miami, Florida, February 1990. I have to rank her as one of the most graceful athletes I've every photographed. Virtually every shot of her in motion she looked good. Rejects were even good. We built a ramp 10 feet long with a huge white wall behind her and a pit of mattresses and foam that she would dive on. She would run on the platform, someone would toss her the ball, and she would do a flying header. Again, I never met a wall I didn't like. If I can't find one, I bring it. This time I brought my own wall.

Page 151: Kluivert, Milan, Italy, October 1997. An unknown athlete who was a pro player. This was on a Marlboro cigarette shoot.

Page 151: Pro soccer player, Ft. Lauderdale, Florida, May 1990.

Surfing
Page 152: Laird Hamilton, Oahu, Hawaii, January 1995. Taken in a beautiful home you rent for photo shoots. It's like the last of the old Hawaii on the west coast. I brought Laird and Kelly Slater over. This was one of Laird's early guns for tow-in surfing, and Kelly was going off about how good Pipeline was that day—five or six great barrel rides backside. Laird just looks at him and says, Huh, only Pipeline. Laird, one of the best-looking men in all of aquatic sports.

Page 154: Hanalei Bay, Kauai, February 1996. From a chopper.

Page 156: Hanalei Bay, Kauai, February 1996. I went there to cover surfing. I didn't really know much about surfing at the time, but I knew if I got in the chopper and got close enough I'd get good pictures. Which was right, but there's always a problem with surfing: the weather, the winds, the tides, the surf conditions. It's too small, too big. I was there for six weeks and barely got the story done. I got so close to these waves that once the white water went through the cabin in the helicopter, and my feet got wet because we had both doors off. And from the shore the waves were so big that when a wave would come through, the chopper would disappear and everyone on the shore would think we went down.

Page 157: Brian Pecheco, Waikiki, Oahu, August 1989. A young surfer back then. A great-looking kid with wonderful hair. Taken on pier overlooking Waikiki.

Page 158: Tommy Chamberlain, "Middles," Hanalei Bay, Kauai, February 1976.

Page 159: Kelly Slater, Sebastian Inlet, Florida, October 1990. At his home break.

Page 160: Na Pali Coast, Kauai, August 1992. One night, a nice swell, water just splashed off the cliffs. The perfect fan, backlit.

Page 161: Danny Kim, Sandy Beach, Oahu, August 1990. Super boogie-boarder. I guess he didn't want to ride a real board. He said he got hit in the head once. But this guy shredded waves at Sandy Beach like no one you ever saw. Taken during the Day-Glo days. Sandy Beach, the greatest natural water park on the planet among the surfers, the body boarders, and the body surfers.

Page 162: Hanalei Bay, Kauai, February 1976.

Page 163: Kelly Slater, Santa Monica, California February 1995. With the sun dropping and starting to form shadows. Kelly didn't have a logo on his board so he drew it in for us that day because of contractual problems if there was no logo. Not only can he surf, he can play guitar, and he's an artist.

Page 164: The Pipeline, North Shore, Oahu, January 1990. I realized I couldn't outshoot local photographers in the water. They risked their lives. I'd lose mine. I mounted four strobes on a bracket on a chopper at twilight.

Page 165: Kelly Slater, Sebastian Inlet, Florida, October 1990. Post-surf shower. Kelly getting cleaned.

Tennis
Page 166: Michael Chang, Roland Garros, Paris France, June 1989. The beautiful clay courts of Roland Garros. Michael Chang on a changeover during the French Open.

Page 168: Boris Becker, Roland Garros, Paris, June 1989. One of those moments that you dream about when the sky turns black and the sun comes out. You know it's not going to last for more than about five minutes. The sun has a slim pocket and then the whole sky iss going to close out. So you shoot like a madman and hope something good happens in your frame.

Page 170: Bjorn Borg, U.S. Open, Flushing Meadow, New York, September 1978.

Page 171: Jimmy Connors, Santa Barbara, California, December 1991.

Page 172: Chris Everet Lloyd, U.S. Open, Flushing Meadow, New York, September 1981.

Page 173: Martina Navratalova, London, July 1978, Big, strong, a weight-lifter, deadly-fast, she changed the face of women's tennis for ever. Without a doubt, the best player in the world when she was on top, and the best women's player ever, I think.

Page 174, 175: John McEnroe, U.S. Open, Flushing Meadow, New York, September 1980 and Septermber 1979. In 1980, on his home court where he triumphed many times; and a year earlier in 1979, winning the U.S. Open.

Page 176, 177: Steffi Graf, Cabo San Lucas, Mexico, November 1996. Taken for a swim-suit issue of *Sports Illustrated*. She hated her profile. One of the first shots was a profile with her hair slicked back. It was a beautiful picture. I'm sure she still hates it. She complained to her agent, so every time I shot her after this, I'd get slightly off-center, her nose was always straight at the camera. She also hated her legs. I said, You have fantastic legs, I'd give anything to have a set of legs like that. I don't know what she liked about herself, but, surprisingly, it wasn't her physique.

Track and Field
Page 178: Carl Lewis, Houston, Texas, May 1988. Taken at his home track. He had many looks over the years. He was always an interesting man to photograph.

Page 180: Carl Lewis, Houston, Texas, September 1991. I built a ramp 24-feet long and five feet off the ground so I could get a solo shot of anything I wanted. This was coming out of the starting blocks, about a stride removed, with a blue filter, and very warm gel on the strobe to create that coloration.

Page 181: Carl Lewis, Houston, Texas, May 1988.

Page 182: Carl Lewis, Houston, Texas, September 1991. For the "Living Legends" series. Carl was, without a doubt, the best track and field athlete ever in running and long jumping, and a wonderful man to photograph.

Page 183: Gail Devers, U.C.L.A., Los Angeles, California, March 1996. Black-and-white Polaroid. What can I say? Look at that amazing face, those legs, those nails.

Page 184: Evelyn Ashford, Indianapolis, Indiana, June 1996. After a race. Just one of those moments when you can't help but notice.

Page 185: Jackie Joyner, Los Angeles, May 1991. My second-favorite female athlete. A person who would just give, give, give—so kind. Sad to see her go out, but it was a beautiful way she went in the '96 Olympics with a bronze metal in the long jump; jumping on one leg and making it on her last jump, the stuff of what champions are made.

Page 186: Starting Line, Los Angeles, California, March 1983. For Adidas. A black and white shoot, but I took one roll of color. I exposed it at 400 ASA instead of 50 so I had to push it, and I'd never pushed 50 that far. It shifted the colors around, but looked beautiful. We had all world-class runners here. To stand in the starting position a long time, the arms start to go and the fingers start to hurt. These guys were moaning and groaning when I kept doing it over and over again.

Page 187: Olympic Trials, Atlanta, Georgia, June 1996.

Page 188: Calvin Smith, Tuscaloosa, Alabama, October 1983 Off the starting blocks. Part of my Fuji Olympics campaign.

Page 189: Edwin Moses, Irvine, California, June 1991. Edwin had retired from hurtles. He was going to make his comeback so he was included in the Legends series for S.I. as the greatest hurdler of all time, which he was. And when we went to his house to get his gear he had no hurtling shoes. The shoes he's wearing are his shoes for the bobsled team he was on. The shoes had little needles coming out that would dig into the ice. They were like razors in the turf of the track. After his first hurtle, Edwin said he was ready to come back. He looked perfect every time. Hadn't done it in two years.

Page 190: Sam Matatae, Auburn, Alabama, March 1992. An exercise to increase the

spring, a form exercise. A canvas behind him to let his shadow mimic his form.

Page 190: Mike Powell, California, April 1991. One of the Olympic series. It was hard to get him in the long jump because they rarely practice. They usually do exercises and form exercises. We finally hooked up on this, a green background down behind the pit. I said, How long you gonna jump? He said, 20, 22 feet. The first jump he jumped 27 feet, one of the longest jumps ever made in history. He took off around the track screaming.

Page 191: Sam Matatae, March 1992. A shot I always try to get, but never really get perfectly; when a runner leans forward as far as he can to stick his head into the electronic tape and throws the arms back.

Page 191: Edwin Moses, Huntington Beach, California, November 1983. I had been trailing a great *Life* magazine photographer at the Olympics. I knew he'd shot Edwin Moses the day before. I was running out of ideas, stalling, didn't know what to do when I got to Edwin. I went into a bathroom. Its outside wall is this background. While I was in there, I saw this shaft of light coming through the opening. I thought of standing him on the urinal—bad way to start the photo session. I went outside and saw the same shaft of light, so I had him stand there right on the edge of the shadow with this beautiful profile. The shadow gave him an African look to his head.

Page 192: Donovan Bailey, Austin, Texas, March 1996. The world's fastest human at the time. Olympic champion at the Atlanta games in '96. I brought my white wall this time on a blustery day. A very moody Donovan was reluctant to do much of anything. Shot for Adidas.

Page 193: Steeplechase, Memorial Coliseum, Los Angeles, 1984 Olympics. A shot every photographer seems to go after because of the pools of water and the reflective qualities of it.

Water
Page 194: Greg Louganis, Mission Viejo, California, February 1984. One of these mystical, magical shots you take once in your career. This was taken at twilight. The sky was black at the top, red at the base of the sky with a half-second exposure as he came off the high platform. The lights that illuminated the pool made the streaks, and the sky—the red and the black—mix together. So when I brought this picture out to show Louganis, I was so proud of myself. I said, Greg look at this, and he said, I'm bent. He handed it back to me and walked away. As you can see, his form at his waist curving back to the left a little, and that was it. I was humiliated by the world's greatest diver.

Page 196: Swimmers, East Germany, June 1976. We went to East Germany with a group of thirteen journalists. We toured in a bus looking for doping of the blood, steroid use. We saw nothing of that. These were two kids at sports college who would spend their lives training virtually all day to make it to the Olympics.

Page 197: Diver, Boca Raton, Florida, June 1990.

Page 198: The Iron Man, Kona, Hawaii, October 1989. This is first light in Kona as the swimmers prepared to take off in the first of three events.

Page 199: Swimmer, Boca Raton, Florida, June 1990. A swimmer off the starting blocks.

Page 200: Swimmer, Los Angeles, California, August 1997. Taken for Adidas, a swimmer coming off the starting blocks.

Page 202: U.S. Synchronized Swim Team, Caracas, Venezuela, August 1983. The team was waiting to enter the pool at the Pan Am Games. They stretched and prepared in front of this retaining wall weathered by the red earth.

Page 203: Todd Torres, Atlantic Olympics, August 1996. It's called the "embryo" when a swimmer breaks the water, but the water doesn't really break on his head, just sort of engulfs it. It's a shot a photographer likes to shoot, but rarely gets.

Page 204: Backstroke Start, 1984 Olympics Games, Los Angeles. Shot with my 14-frame-per-second camera during the heats. There was only one like this.

Page 205: Diver, Olympic Trials, Indianapolis, IN, May 1984.

Page 206: Julia Cruz, Ft. Lauderdale, Florida, January 1994. I put my assistant with a strobe on the platform above her and lit her againstthe gray sky.

Page 207: Paul Barton, Melbourne, Florida February 1992. Here's a picture that's very difficult to make look unusual. I went out in the water and I kept processing each day and never thought I had anything really unique. I must have shot 40 rolls of this guy in days. There was one shot, and this was it. Part of the Olympic series.

Various

Page 208: Nicole Uphoff, Mainz, Germany, January 1992. Taken on a miserable day in Germany with a hot light. I was afraid to use the strobe with a horse. They're so skittish. A horrible 10 days of rain in Germany. But what do you expect in January.

Page 210: Kamala, The Ugandan Giant, New Haven, Connecticut, April 1985. When the W.W.F. hit its new high. I went to New Haven to photograph Kamala, and a group of other people. I asked him to stand behind a palm tree I had there. I said, Can you stand there? His man Friday said Kamala only speaks African. So, I said, Can you ask him to move behind the plant? He says, Oooa, oooa. I'd ask him to move his arm—Oooa, ooooha—and he'd move his arm. Great actors.

Page 211: The Alaskans, New Haven, Connecticut, April 1985. Here are the Alaskans, or the baked Alaskans, another bunch of freaks, but they were very amusing characters.

Page 212: Steve Rottman, Santa Monica, California, January 1993. I had a cherry picker. What struck me was the way the sand looked with the angle of light cutting across it. He had beautiful form. He almost looked like an eagle taking off, the way he strode into his jump serve.

Page 213: Chuck Dinkins, Key Biscayne, Florida This was an ad shoot for Gatorade. We built a ramp for this skateboarder. He made two jumps like this and almost fractured his knee. He ended up in the hospital. Very short shoot, very nervous clients.

Page 214: Willy Shoemaker, Hollywood Park, Hollywood, California, December 1988. This was taken for a story that never ran in *S.I.* called "The end of the game." It was how athletes looked at the end of combat or competition. This was after a muddy day with the great Willy Shoemaker.

Acknowledgments

Many people have told me that I've led a charmed life and held one of the world's best jobs. And, honestly, I can't argue: it's been a fantastic ride. But what I've been truly and most blessed with is Eva Iooss, my one and only. Being married to a photographer can't be easy, with all the constant travel. With Eva's help, we've maintained a stable and treasured family life.
Since 1961 *Sports Illustrated* has been a second home to me, and many people there have had a profound effect on my career. The first was George Bloodgood, a picture editor, who saw something in me, a kid with braces from New Jersey. He opened the door and let me in. Thanks to Andre Laguerre, the great Managing Editor. To Gil Rogin who published some of my best essays in the early 1980s. Heinz Kleutmeier and Karen Mullarky who brought me back to the magazine in the late 1980s, and Steve Fine, the current picture editor, who has given me the chance to piece together my career and close it where it began. John Zimmerman, the great *S.I.* shooter, largely inspired me and taught me not only photography but a few lessons on the tennis court. Neil Leifer, my friend and one time rival who showed me there was more to life than a party. He will forever and always push the limits. Thanks to Alfred Eisenstadt who in my eyes was the spiritual father to all *Time* and *Life* photographers. (I believe there is a piece of Eisie in all of us). To Jule Campbell for plucking an immature sports photographer from the arenas and putting him on the beach with the *S.I.* swimsuit models. Mark Vaneil and "Rare Air." Marty Pedersen's great patience and design for this book. To Peter Beard and The Queen Annie Leibovitz who are constant inspirations to me. To all my favorite athletes who have shared their time with me, listed here in no particular order: Bjorn Borg, Art Mahaffey, Chris Evert, Dick Allen, Michael Jordan and his family, Johnny Unitas, Joe Montana, Mario Andretti, Kelly Slater, Junior Griffey, Jackie Joyner-Kersee, Willie Stargell, Brett Farve, Magic Johnson, Kobe Bryant, Scotty Pippen, and Cal Ripkin, Jr. Finally, the best for last. My father who lit the flame, my mother whose devotion is unmatched, and my sons, Christian and Bjorn, who mean the world to me and may yet take the torch from me one day.
Thanks to all of you. *Walter Iooss*

WALTER IOOSS

(Photographs from 1958 to 1998)

Walter Iooss shoots with Canon cameras on Fuji film